A Banquet

for Cecilia

How Cecilia Chiang Revolutionized Chinese Food in America

By Julie Leung

Illustrated by Melissa Iwai

Little, Brown and Company
New York Boston

*I*magine you are little Cecilia Chiang,
the seventh daughter in a large and wealthy Chinese family.
You live in an old palace in Beijing,
one that contains fifty-two rooms
and stretches across an entire city block.

Imagine you are Cecilia peering
into her most favorite room of all—
the kitchen!

She heard such interesting noises!

Sharp cleavers went *thunk, thunk, thunk* on wooden blocks.

Hot oil sizzled in big metal woks.

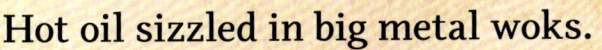

Hot steam whistled out of bamboo baskets. And the voices of her family's two chefs mingled together as they prepared elaborate meals for her parents, Cecilia, and all her brothers and sisters!

Cecilia was not allowed inside the kitchen. But, oh, the most delightful smells drifted out! Savory soy sauce and scallions made her stomach gurgle. Fried garlic and tangy vinegar made her mouth water. Red chilies and numbing peppers tickled the inside of her nose.

When it was time to eat, her father would be served first in the dining room.

When the children were finally allowed in, her father noted the details that made each dish perfect: A dumpling wrapper must be rolled thick enough to hold its shape but also thin enough to not be too chewy. A fish should be sliced at diagonal angles to allow the sauce to seep in evenly. Just a pinch of salt could bring out the sweetness of a mantou, a fluffy white steamed bun.

小籠包
Xiǎo lóng bāo

From the family's native Shanghai: round pork dumplings, plump with soup inside. Cecilia bit into them slowly so the broth wouldn't squirt out.

京醬肉絲
Jīng jiàng ròu sī

A local Beijing specialty: shredded pork sautéed in soybean paste. Cecilia scooped the meat onto a thin piece of tofu skin and folded it into a roll to eat.

紅豆湯
Hóng dòu tāng

Served cold in the summer and hot in the winter: a sweet soup made from red beans. Cecilia always found room in her stomach for this dessert.

Cecilia's father wanted all his daughters to be educated,
which was very rare in 1930s China.

But when the Japanese invaded Beijing in 1937, Cecilia's future darkened in the shadow of war. By 1943, she knew her opportunities lay elsewhere.

Cecilia and one of her sisters decided to take the perilous trip to Chongqing, where the Chinese capital had relocated. It was over one thousand miles away.

Surviving on a few gold coins sewn into their clothes, they traveled by foot alongside thousands fleeing the city. Cecilia and her sister walked only at night to avoid being spotted by fighter planes.

When they heard the ferocious, roaring engines overhead, they would run into nearby sorghum fields to hide from gunfire. It took them nearly six months to reach Chongqing.

During their journey, Cecilia passed through many regions of China.
The Beijing accent she'd heard all her life faded the farther she traveled.
She saw how cuisine also changed from province to province, town to town.

Such a vast country, Cecilia marveled.
So many different cooking styles.

Beijing

HEBEI

SHANDONG

SHAANXI

Kaifeng Shangqiu

Xi'an Xuzhou

HENAN Jieshou

SICHUAN

Chongqing

回鍋肉
Huí guō ròu
Twice-cooked pork

N
W   E
S

打滷麵
Dǎ lǔ miàn
Very thick hot-and-sour noodles

豆沙包
Dòu shā bāo
Sweet red bean bun

After World War II ended, Cecilia got married. Together, she and her husband resettled in Shanghai and had a baby.

However, a civil war soon consumed her country. In 1949, Cecilia and her family escaped on the last plane to Tokyo.

She would not be able to return to China
or see her family, who remained behind,
for many, many years.

Missing the food of her home country, Cecilia helped open a Chinese restaurant called the Forbidden City. Cecilia served her favorite Shanghainese dishes.

One day, she received a letter from a
younger sister who had moved to America.
Her sister was lonely in her new country and
wanted company. Cecilia agreed to go stay with her.

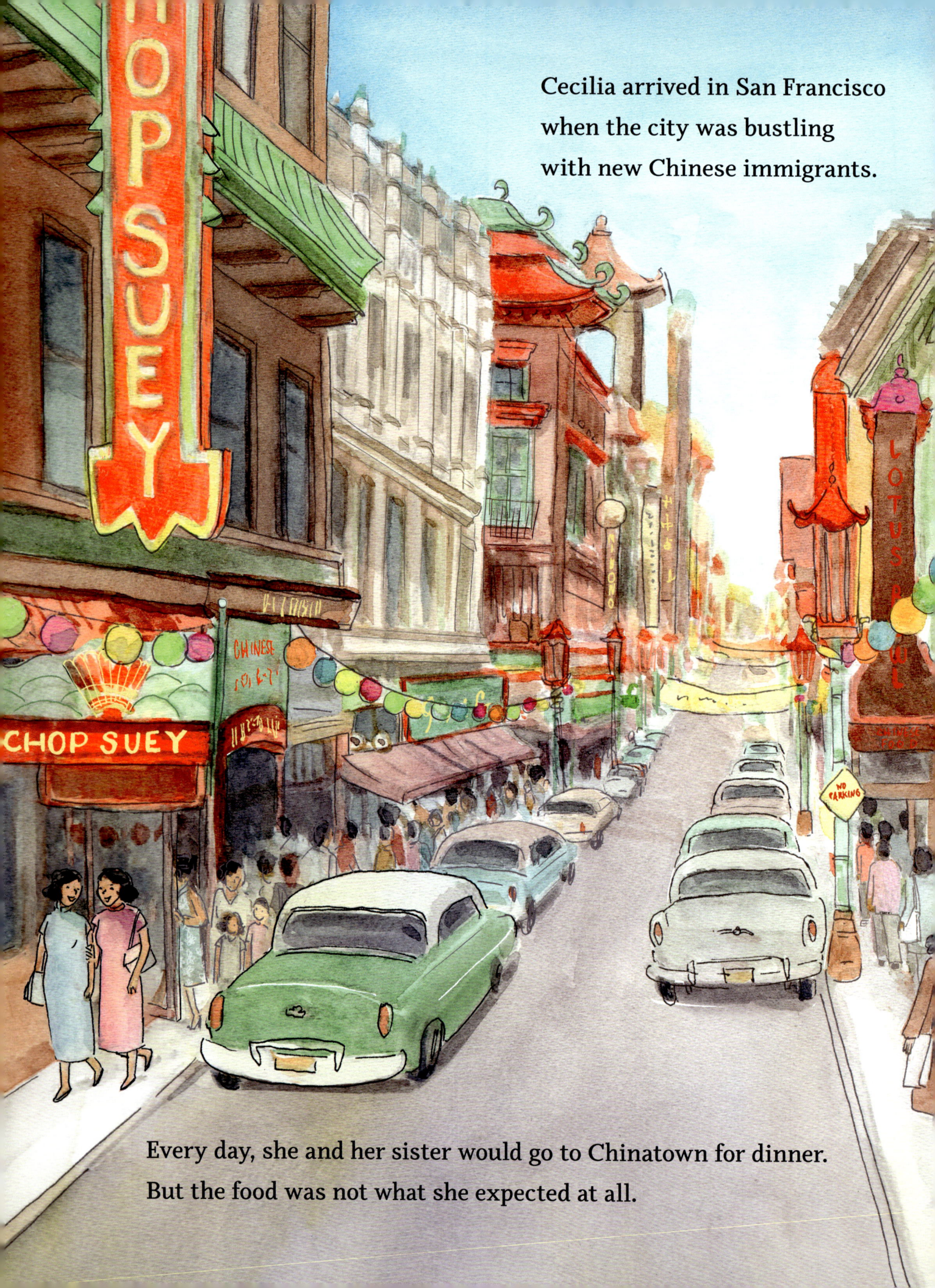

Cecilia arrived in San Francisco
when the city was bustling
with new Chinese immigrants.

Every day, she and her sister would go to Chinatown for dinner.
But the food was not what she expected at all.

炒麵
Chow mein
Stir-fried egg noodles

芙蓉蛋
Egg foo yong
Panfried omelets

雜碎
Chop suey
A meat and vegetable stir-fry that translates to "a little bit of this and that"

Cecilia was disappointed. This was nothing like the food back home. What a shame that Chinese food in America was considered cheap, fast dining. "Chinese food is not just chop suey," she complained to her sister.

One morning, she ran into two friends from Tokyo.
"Cecilia, can you help us?" they asked.
They wanted to open a restaurant and needed someone to
translate between them and the landlord. Cecilia agreed to help.
When the landlord asked for rental money, she paid it herself.

But when it came time to start planning the restaurant,
her friends decided they didn't want to open one after all.
Cecilia was suddenly stuck with the building!

She didn't want to quit or tell her husband what had happened. She remembered the beautifully prepared banquets of her childhood. She imagined how she might transform this place into a palace. "Well, I guess I'm going to open the restaurant, then!" she decided.

Cecilia created a menu of over two hundred dishes that would showcase the best flavors from China's many regions.

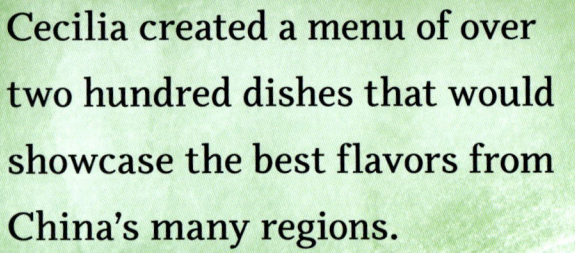

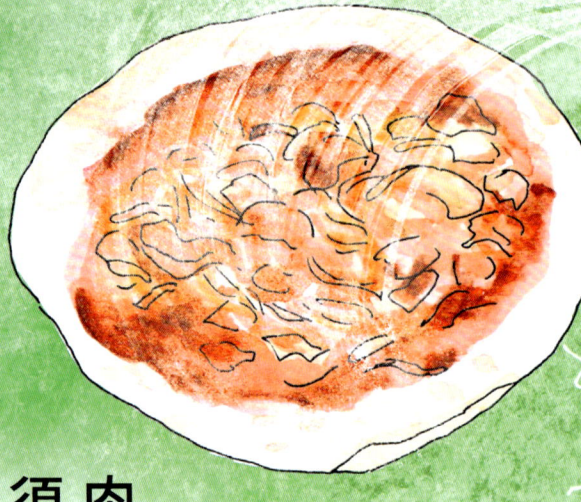

木須肉
Moo shu pork from Shandong
Sliced pork sautéed with wood ear mushrooms, bean sprouts, and eggs, served with flour pancakes for wrapping and hoisin sauce, a soybean-based sauce, for dipping

SICHUAN

麻婆豆腐
Mapo tofu from Sichuan
Tofu served with minced meat, floating in a spicy, oily stew of chilies and peppercorns

獅子頭

Lion's head meatballs from Shanghai

Braised pork meatballs served with napa cabbage,
so that they resemble a lion's head and mane

SHANDONG

SHANGHAI

On the bright red cover of her menu, she
printed the name of her new restaurant:
the Mandarin.

the
MANDARIN

When the Mandarin opened in 1961, Cecilia served her food on quality plates and fine white tablecloths. She trained her waiters to explain the origins of each dish. And whenever Cecilia traveled to Asia, she brought back hard-to-find ingredients.

To make ends meet in the first few years, Cecilia doubled as the dishwasher and mopped the kitchen herself.

Many food suppliers would not sell to her, thinking her restaurant was doomed. They laughed at the menu and prices.

"Why would you charge that kind of money when you could get Chinese food for so much less?"

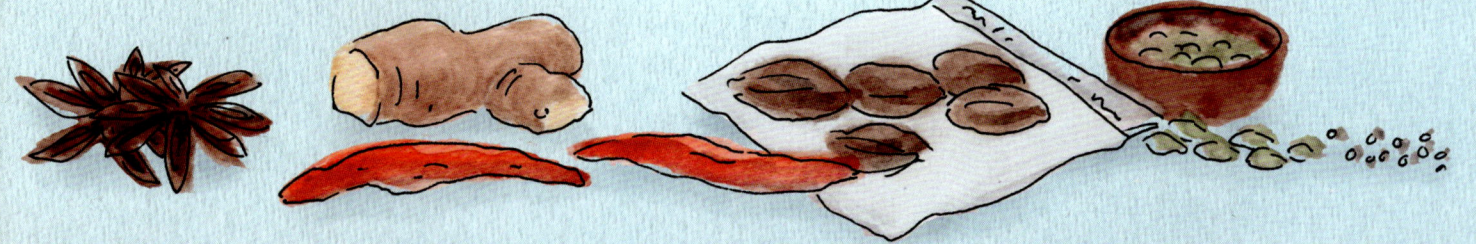

One day, a man came in and ordered some panfried dumplings.

"These taste just like the ones I had in Beijing!" he exclaimed.

The next time, he brought a friend who was a newspaper columnist.

The columnist wrote a glowing restaurant review.

"The best Chinese food east of the Pacific," it proclaimed.

Suddenly, the Mandarin was the talk of San Francisco!

樟茶鴨
Tea-smoked duck

Duck that has been marinated in spices for hours and then smoked with black tea leaves

叫花雞
Beggar's chicken

A stuffed chicken wrapped in lotus leaves and encased in clay, slow-roasted for hours until tender

回鍋肉
Twice-cooked pork

Pork belly simmered in spices and chilled, then sliced and stir-fried with bell peppers and onions

The restaurant became so popular, Cecilia expanded to a bigger location. In the decades that followed, rock stars and politicians alike dined at the Mandarin. She fed everyone from the Beatles to the king of Denmark.

Chefs would come from all over to learn how to prepare the Mandarin's food, and other Chinese restaurants began adopting dishes that Cecilia helped make popular.

During a time when Chinese food in America was seen as cheap and greasy, Cecilia Chiang served dishes that showcased the best of her homeland. She encouraged her diners to be open to something new and different.

Her first menu at the Mandarin included this introduction:
"Imagine you are a Chinese family . . ."

It was a simple but revolutionary ask: to put yourself in someone
else's shoes—perhaps a seventh daughter who once lived in a
palace, peering into the kitchen to see the banquet emerge.

AUTHOR'S NOTE

*T*he menu at my parents' Chinese restaurant, in Georgia, was very typical of what you would find in any average American town today: General Tso's chicken, wonton soup, egg foo young. Even as a kid running the cash register, I knew there was a big difference between these fast, casual (and still delicious!) stir-fry menu items and *authentic* Chinese cooking, which varies immensely across the regions of China and can be stunningly complex to prepare.

A Banquet for Cecilia only delves into a small fraction of the dishes that Cecilia Chiang helped make popular through her restaurant in San Francisco, the Mandarin. (The original menu featured two hundred items!) In presenting this dazzling array of seafood, meats, grains, and more to you, I've made intentional style changes as the story progresses from Cecilia's childhood to her years as a famous restauranteur. At the beginning of Cecilia's story, the English is a pinyin guide to how the food would have been pronounced in Mandarin. However, when Cecilia arrives in San Francisco's Chinatown, the dishes are simply written as they would have been known in the United States. For instance, the "foo young" in "egg foo young" is essentially a transliteration of the Cantonese

Young Cecilia in China.

Cecilia on the ship coming to
the United States.

pronunciation of 芙蓉, or "fu⁴ jung⁴," and the shorter food descriptions serve as a counterpoint to the more complex dishes Cecilia introduced to the West. Lastly, the foods at the end of the book were pulled from Cecilia's own cookbooks. For these, I stayed true to how she herself named these dishes.

Through Cecilia Chiang and the Mandarin, Americans were introduced to China's diversity of flavors and cooking styles. She presented Chinese cuisine as a fine-dining experience—worthy of Western media reviews and awards—and pioneered a culinary awakening in this country.

Cecilia in her home kitchen, outside San Francisco, California.

For my mother, who always asks if I've eaten yet —JL

For my son, Jamie, who, thanks to Cecilia, has been able to taste and fall in love with all the amazing cuisines of China —MI

ABOUT THIS BOOK

The illustrations for this book were done in watercolor, ink, and digital tools on Fabriano hot press watercolor paper. This book was edited by Farrin Jacobs and Nikki Garcia and designed by Angelie Yap. The production was supervised by Lillian Sun, and the production editor was Marisa Finkelstein. The text was set in Odile and Adorn Roman, and the display type was hand-lettered.